Twenty to Make
Knitted Flowers

Susie Johns

Search Press

First published in Great Britain 2010

Search Press Limited
Wellwood, North Farm Road,
Tunbridge Wells, Kent TN2 3DR

Reprinted 2010, 2011

Text copyright © Susie Johns 2010

Photographs by Roddy Paine Photographic Studios

Photographs and design copyright
© Search Press Ltd 2010

ISBN: 978-1-84448-493-5

Suppliers
If you have difficulty in obtaining any of the
materials and equipment mentioned in this book,
then please visit the Search Press website for
details of suppliers: www.searchpress.com

Printed in Malaysia

Abbreviations

beg: beginning

inc: increase (by working into the front and
back of the stitch)

k: knit

k2tog: knit two stitches together

knitwise: as though to knit

p: purl

p2tog: purl two stitches together

psso: pass slipped stitch over

rem: remaining

rep: repeat

sl: slip, usually slip 1 stitch

st(s): stitch(es)

tbl: through back loop

WS: wrong side

*: repeat the instructions following the * as
many times as specified

Contents

Introduction

Cunningly crafted yet surprisingly quick and easy to make, this colourful collection of flowers is just the thing to use up oddments of yarn. Use them to decorate hats, hairbands, scarves, jackets, coats or cardigans; pin or stitch them to a bag, or use them to decorate household items such as cushions and tea cosies.

Whether you are a novice knitter, daunted by difficult patterns or a veteran who is eager to take a break from bigger projects, there is plenty here to occupy fidgety fingers.

Knitters have a tendency to accumulate yarn – leftovers from larger projects, sale purchases, donations or swaps – and if you search your stash you will no doubt find enough oddments to make a start. Then next time you go shopping, treat yourself to a ball of green double knitting for some stems and perhaps some yellow bouclé or an eye-catching eyelash yarn for a bold centre or some sensational stamens. Tapestry yarns and novelty embroidery threads can also be introduced.

On a technical note, unless otherwise stated, right and wrong sides of work are interchangeable: just decide which side of the flower or petal looks best, or base your decision on which way the petals curl. Tension (or gauge) is not given: just aim for a firm fabric that will hold its shape, using a smaller needle than the one stated in the pattern, if necessary, to produce the right result.

Some of the patterns, such as the Daffodil and Arum Lily, require you to knit in the round on double-pointed needles, so if you find the idea too challenging, start with one of the easier projects such as the Cosmos, Daisy, Tulip, Anemone or Cactus Flower. If you prefer a challenge, however, then head straight for the Periwinkle and Sweet William – though the seasoned knitter will find these simple, I am sure.

The flowers

Water Lily, page 8

Zinnia, page 10

Cactus Flower, page 12

Pansy, page 14

Daffodil, page 16

Peace Lily, page 18

Grape Hyacinth, page 20

Cosmos, page 22

Hibiscus, page 24

Clematis, page 26

Sweet William, page 28

Poppy, page 30

Chrysanthemum, page 32

Tulip, page 34

Periwinkle, page 36

Anemone, page 38

Cherry Blossom, page 40

Arum Lily, page 42

Daisy, page 44

Rose, page 46

Water Lily

Materials:

Double knitting yarn, bright pink

Polyester double knitting yarn, bright yellow

Needles:

1 pair 3.00mm (UK 11; US 2) knitting needles

Tapestry needle

Measurements:

Finished flower measures 12cm (4¾in) across

Instructions:

Outer flower

Cast on 9 sts.

Row 1: k all sts tbl.

Row 2: k.

Row 3: inc 1, k to end (10 sts).

Row 4: k.

Row 5: inc 1, k to end (11 sts).

Row 6: k.

Row 7: inc 1, k to end (12 sts).

Row 8: k.

Row 9: k2tog, k to end (11 sts).

Row 10: k.

Row 11: k2tog, k to end (10 sts).

Row 12: k.

Row 13: k2tog, k to end (9 sts).

Row 14: k.

Row 15: cast off 6, k to end.

Row 16: k3, cast on 6 (8 sts).

Rep rows 1–16 three times more and rows 1–14 once, then cast off all sts; break yarn and fasten off.

Inner flower

Cast on 8 sts.

Row 1: k all sts tbl.

Row 2: k.

Row 3: inc 1, k to end (9 sts).

Row 4: k.

Row 5: inc 1, k to end (10 sts).

Next 3 rows: k.

Row 9: k2tog, k to end (9 sts).

Row 10: k.

Row 11: k2tog, k to end (8 sts).

Row 12: k.

Row 13: cast off 5, k to end.

Row 14: k3, cast on 5 (8 sts).

Rep rows 1–14 twice more and rows 1–12 once, then cast off all sts; break yarn and fasten off.

Centre

Cast on 6 sts.

Row 1: cast off 5 sts, turn.

Row 2: cast on 5 sts.

Rep rows 1 and 2 seven times more, then cast off all sts; break yarn and fasten off.

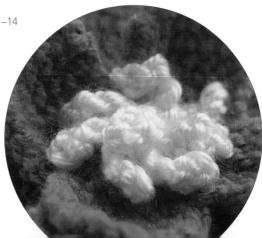

Making up

Join the two ends of the outer flower by stitching the lower corners of the two end petals together, then run a thread along the base of all the petals and pull up tightly to gather; do the same with the inner flower and the flower centre. Stitch the inner flower on top of the outer flower, matching centres. Stitch the flower centre in place.

The deep pink water lily could make a big, bold corsage to wear on a winter coat or a felt hat or beret. To knit the pale pink alternative, make up the flower using a textured pale pink yarn and make the flower centre with an acid yellow mohair yarn for a textural contrast.

Zinnia

Materials:

Mohair yarn, yellow-green

Eyelash yarn, rainbow

Round button, 23mm (⅞in)

Small, sharp scissors

Needles:

1 pair 2.75mm (UK 12; US 2) knitting needles

Tapestry needle

Instructions:

Petals (in one piece)

With two strands of main yarn and 2.75mm (UK 12; US 2) needles, cast on 12 sts.

Row 1: k all sts tbl.

Row 2: k.

Row 3: inc 1, k to end (13 sts).

Row 4: k.

Row 5: inc 1, k to end (14 sts).

Row 6: k.

Row 7: k2tog, k to end (11 sts).

Row 8: k.

Row 9: k2tog, k to end (10 sts).

Row 10: k.

Row 11: k2tog, k to end (9 sts).

Row 12: k.

Row 13: cast off 10, k to end.

Row 14: k2, cast on 10 (12 sts).

Rep rows 1–14 four times more and rows 1–12 once, then cast off all sts; break yarn and fasten off.

Centre

With eyelash yarn and 2.75mm needles, cast on 12 sts and work 20 rows in garter stitch (k every row), then cast off; break yarn and fasten off.

Measurements:

Finished flower measures 14.5cm (5¾in) across

Note:

For knitting petals, use yarn double.

Making up

Bring the two edges of the knitting together to make a circle of petals and stitch the lower corners of the two end petals together. Run a gathering stitch around the centre, along the base of each petal and pull up tightly to gather.

Run a gathering stitch all round the edge of the centre, place the button inside and pull up tightly to gather up and enclose the button.

Stitch the flower centre firmly in place.

With small, sharp scissors, trim away strands of yarn from the top surface of the flower centre, close to the knitted stitches (be careful not to cut the stitches), leaving strands radiating out from the sides only.

This big, bold flower makes a great decoration for a winter coat or wrap, or to add a splash of colour to a plain cardigan. Petals knitted in a pink-violet shade of mohair yarn, with the same rainbow yarn in the centre, create a very exotic bloom.

Cactus Flower

Materials:

Pale green mohair yarn
Polyester double knitting yarn, bright yellow
Pure wool double knitting yarn, brown
Novelty chenille thread, bright pink
Flower pot, 10cm (4in) in diameter
Scrap of stiff card
Polyester wadding or toy stuffing
Fabric glue or all-purpose adhesive (optional)

Measurements:

Finished flower measures 6cm (2³⁄₈in) across
and cactus measures 8cm (3¹⁄₈in) high

Instructions:

Cactus

With mohair yarn and size 3.00mm (UK 11;
US 2) double-pointed needles, cast on 8 sts
and distribute between four needles.
Round 1: k.
Round 2: inc in each st (16 sts).
Round 3: (inc 1, k3) 4 times (20 sts).
Round 4: (inc 1, k4) 4 times (24 sts).
Round 5: (inc 1, k5) 4 times (28 sts).
Round 5: (inc 1, k6) 4 times (32 sts).
Knit 15 rounds without further increases.
Round 21: (k2tog, k6) 4 times (28 sts).
Knit 5 rounds.
Round 27: (k2tog, k5) 4 times (24 sts).
Knit 9 rounds.
Cast off; break yarn and fasten off.

Flower (in one piece)

With yellow yarn and size 2.25mm
(UK 13; US 1) needles, cast on 9 sts.
Row 1: k all sts tbl.
Row 2: p6, turn.
Row 3: k to end.

Needles:

Set of 5 double-pointed knitting needles,
  3.00mm (UK 11; US 2)
1 pair 2.25mm (UK 13; US 1) knitting needles
Tapestry needle

Row 4: p.
Row 5: cast off 7 sts knitwise, k rem st.
Row 6: k2, cast on 7 sts.
Rep rows 1–6 four times more, then rep rows
1–4 once; cast off all sts knitwise; break yarn
and fasten off.

Earth

With brown DK yarn used double and two size
3.00mm needles, cast on 8 sts.
Row 1: k.
Row 2: inc 1, k to end.
Rep last row until
there are 20 sts.
Knit 8 rows
without further
increases.
Cast off 1 st
at beg of next
12 rows.
Cast off rem
8 sts; break yarn
and fasten off.

Making up

Cut a circle of stiff card 9cm (3½in) in diameter.

Stitch a gathering thread all round the edge of the brown piece of knitting (earth), place the card circle centrally on the wrong side and pull up thread to gather; fasten off.

Stuff the cactus firmly with polyester wadding. Using matching green yarn, stitch the base of the cactus to the earth.

Bring the two edges of the flower petals together to make a circle and stitch the lower corners of the two end petals together; then run a gathering stitch along the base of the petals and pull up tightly to gather. Stitch a few strands of pink chenille thread in the centre of the flower, then stitch the flower in place on top of the cactus.

Finally, wedge the whole thing into the top of a flower pot or small ornamental bucket; glue in place if you wish.

These exotic novelty knits are great for decorating windowsills, whatever the season. For the alternative cactus, use an emerald green linen slub yarn and make up the flower in a red pure wool double knitting yarn with a centre made from rainbow eyelash yarn.

Pansy

Materials:
Pure wool double knitting yarn, violet,
   pink-violet and yellow

Measurements:
Finished flower measures 11cm (4³/₈in) across

Needles:
1 pair 3.00mm (UK 11; US 2) knitting needles
Tapestry needle

Instructions:
Plain petal
With violet yarn and size 3.00mm
(UK 11; US 2) needles, cast on 5 sts.

Row 1: inc in each st to end (10 sts).

Row 2: k.

Row 3: inc in each st to end (20 sts).

Row 4: k.

Row 5: inc in each st to end (40 sts).

Knit 3 rows.

Cast off; break yarn and fasten off.

Two-colour petal
With pink-violet yarn and 3.00mm needles, cast
on 5 sts and work rows 1 to 3; break yarn.

Join in violet yarn and work pattern from row 4
to end.

Three-colour petal
With yellow yarn and 3.00mm needles, cast on
5 sts and work row 1; break yarn.

Join in violet-pink yarn and work rows 2 and 3;
break yarn.

Join in violet yarn and work pattern from
row 4 to end.

Making up
Fold each petal in half with right sides together
and stitch cast-on edge and sides to form
a central seam.

Place the two three-colour petals right sides
together and stitch two edges together.
Open out.

Place the two two-colour petals on top,
overlapping slightly, and stitch in place.

Place the plain petal behind the other petals to
form the top of the flower and stitch in place.

Finally, with spare yellow yarn, embroider
4 chain stitches from centre to base of each
three-colour petal and a few straight stitches in
the centre of the flower.

Stitch your knitted pansies to an old-fashioned tea cosy for a touch of nostalgia, or to the ends of a scarf, or make a brooch to decorate your knitwear. Experiment with other colour combinations, such as pink-violet petals with claret centres and the same yellow detail as the main flower. In the background flower here, the 'wrong' sides of the petals have been used, creating a slightly different effect.

Daffodil

Materials:

Silk double knitting yarn, yellow
Pure wool double knitting yarn, green
Pipe cleaner, 28cm (11in)
Round button, 21mm (8¼in)

Measurements:

Finished flower measures 12cm (4¾in) across
and 16cm (6¼in) high

Instructions:

Trumpet

With yellow silk yarn and 3.00mm (UK 11;
US 2) double-pointed needles, cast on 8 sts
and divide equally between four needles.

Round 1: k.

Round 2: inc in each st (16 sts).

Round 3: k.

Round 4: (inc 1, k3) 4 times (20 sts).

Round 5: k.

Round 6: (inc 1, k4) 4 times (24 sts).

Knit 15 rounds without further increases.

Round 21: inc in each st (48 sts).

Cast off; break yarn and fasten off.

Petals (make 6)

With yellow silk yarn and 3.00mm needles, cast
on 7 sts.

Row 1: p3, inc 2, p3 (9 sts).

Row 2: k3, p3, k3.

Row 3: p3, inc 1, k1, inc 1, p3 (11 sts).

Row 4: k3, p5, k3.

Row 5: p3, k5, p3.

Row 6: k3, p5, k3.

Row 7: p3, k2tog tbl, k1, k2tog, p3 (9 sts).

Row 8: k3, p3, k3.

Row 9: p3, sl1, k2tog, psso, p3 (7 sts).

Row 10: k3, p1, k3.

Needles:

Set of 5 double-pointed
knitting needles,
3.00mm (UK 11; US 2)

1 pair 3.00mm
(UK 11; US 2)
knitting needles

Tapestry needle

Row 11: p2, p3tog, p2 (5 sts).

Row 12: k.

Row 13: p1, p3tog, p1 (3 sts).

Row 14: k.

Row 15: p3tog; break yarn and fasten off.

Stalk

With green yarn and two double-pointed
needles, cast on 5 sts.

Row 1: k5; do not turn but slide sts to other end
of needle.

Rep this row until work measures 26cm;
fasten off.

Leaf

Follow instructions for stalk until work measures 3cm (1¼in), then work in rows as follows:

Next row: inc 1, k3, inc 1 (7 sts).

Next row: k2, p3, k2.

Next row: k.

Rep last 2 rows until work measures 20cm (7⅞in), ending with a knit row.

Next row: k2tog, k1, p1, k1, k2tog (5 sts).

Next row: k.

Next row: k2tog, k1, k2tog (3 sts).

Next row: sl1, k2tog, psso; break yarn and fasten off.

Making up

Stitch the lower corners of the petals together so that the petals form a ring. Run a gathering stitch around the base of the petals and pull up slightly, so that the base of the trumpet fits inside. Stitch the trumpet in place. To help keep its shape, stitch a button inside the base of the trumpet, if you wish.

Fold over 5mm (¼in) at either end of the pipe cleaner and slip it inside the stalk. Stitch the ends of the stalk closed. Stitch the top of the stalk to the base of the trumpet. Stitch the leaf in place about a third of the way up the stem.

Make the daffodil in 2-ply Shetland yarn, using the yarn double to achieve a firm result. Make the trumpet in a rich shade of yellow and the petals in a paler shade. To make the stalk more supportive, insert a wooden skewer instead of a pipe cleaner.

Peace Lily

Materials:
Cotton/acrylic double knitting yarn, white
Acrylic double knitting bouclé yarn, yellow
Pure wool double knitting yarn, green

Measurements:
Finished flower is 15cm (6in) long,
    including stem

Needles:
1 pair 3.00mm (UK 11; US 2) knitting needles
2 double-pointed 3.00mm (UK 11; US 2)
    knitting needles
Tapestry needle

Instructions:
With white yarn and size 3.00mm (UK 11; US 2)
needles, cast on 9 sts.

Row 1: k.

Row 2: k1, p7, k1.

Row 3: k1, (inc 1, k1) 4 times (13 sts).

Row 4: k1, p11, k1.

Row 5: k1, (inc 1, k1) 6 times, k1 (19 sts).

Row 6: k1, p17, k1.

Row 7: k1, (inc 1) 17 times, k1 (35 sts)

Row 8: k1, p33, k1.

Row 9: k.

Rep rows 8 and 9 three times.

Rep row 8 once.

Row 17: (k2, k2tog) 4 times, k4, (sl 1, k1, psso,
k2) 4 times (28 sts).

Row 18: k1, p26, k1.

Row 19: (k2, k2tog) 3 times, k4 (sl 1, k1, psso,
k2) 3 times (22 sts).

Row 20: k1, p20, k1.

Row 21: (k2, k2tog) twice, k6, (sl 1, k1, psso, k2)
twice (18 sts).

Row 22: k1, p16, k1.

Row 23: (k2, k2tog) twice, k2, (sl 1, k1, psso, k2)
twice (14 sts).

Row 24: k1, p12, k1.

Row 25: k2, k2tog, k2tog, sl 1, k1, psso, k2tog,
sl 1, k1, psso, k2 (9 sts).

Row 26: k1, p7, k1.

Row 27: k1, k2tog, sl 1, k1, psso, k1, sl 1, k1,
psso, k1 (6 sts).

Row 28: k1, p2tog tbl, p2tog, k1 (4 sts).

Row 29: k1, sl 2, k1, psso (2 sts).

Row 30: p2tog; break yarn and fasten off.

Spadix
With yellow bouclé yarn and size 3.00mm
needles, cast on 16 sts, knit 5 rows and cast off;
break yarn and fasten off.

Stem

With green yarn and two double-pointed needles, cast on 5 sts.

Row 1: k5; do not turn but slide sts to other end of needle.

Rep this row until work measures 7cm (2¾in); fasten off.

Making up

To form the spadix, fold under 1.5cm (¾in) at one end, then slip stitch the long edges together to make a firm tube. Stitch the narrower end to the top of the stem. Place inside the flower, positioning the join at the base of the flower and stitch, wrapping the cast-on edge around to hide the join.

Pin or stitch the lily to a bag or purse, or a jacket lapel. Instead of white, you could knit the main part of the flower in a deep coral pink cotton double knitting yarn.

Grape Hyacinth

Materials:

Chinese silk yarn, bright purple
Pure wool double knitting yarn, green

Measurements:

Finished flower is 14.5cm (5¾in) long,
    including stem

Needles:

1 pair 3.25mm (UK 10; US 3) knitting needles,
2 double-pointed 3.00mm (UK 11; US 2)
    knitting needles
Tapestry needle

Instructions:

To make a bobble (mb)

Knit into front and back of stitch, turn; k3, turn;
k3, turn; pass 2nd and 3rd stitches over 1st
stitch, then slip this stitch back on to right-hand
needle; turn.

Flower

With silk yarn and 3.25mm (UK 10; US 3)
needles, cast on 15 sts.

Row 1: *mb, k3, rep from * to end.

Row 2: p.

Row 3: k2, (mb, k3) 4 times, k1.

Row 4: p .

Rep rows 1–4 once, then rep rows 1 and 2 once;
cast off all sts knitwise; break yarn and
fasten off.

Stem

With green yarn and two double-pointed
needles, cast on 2 sts.

Row 1: k2; do not turn but slide sts to other end
of needle.

Rep this row until work measures 6.5cm (2½in);
fasten off.

Making up

Place the cast-off edge of the flower over the
cast-on edge, overlapping slightly, and slip
stitch it in place. Stitch the three bobbles at the
top of the flower together in a cluster. Insert
the end of the stem into the base of the flower
and stitch it in place.

*To make a lapel
pin, use matching
yarn to stitch
a brooch pin
to the slip-
stitched
seam.*

Hyacinths could be used singly or in a bunch, as a lapel pin on a jacket. Use a textured, variegated yarn in pink/purple for an alternative; if it is slightly thicker, the resulting flower will be larger, even if you use the same size needles.

Cosmos

Materials:

Lightweight pure wool double knitting yarn, deep pink and yellow

Tapestry wool, red

Round button, 12mm (½in)

Measurements:

Finished flower measures 9cm (3½in) across

Needles:

1 pair 2.75mm (UK 12; US 2) knitting needles

Tapestry needle

Instructions:

Petal (make 8)

With deep pink yarn and size 2.75mm (UK 12; US 2) needles, cast on 2 sts.

Knit 2 rows.

Row 3: (inc 1) twice (4 sts).

Knit 5 rows.

Next row: k1, (inc 1) twice, k1 (6 sts).

Knit 5 rows.

Next row: k1, (k2tog) twice, k1 (2 sts).

Knit 2 rows.

Cast off, break yarn and fasten off.

Centre

With yellow yarn and 2.75mm needles, cast on 2 sts.

Row 1: inc 1, k to end.

Rep last row until there are 8 sts.

Knit 3 rows.

Next row: cast off 1, k to end.

Rep last row until there are 2 sts.

Cast off; break yarn and fasten off.

Making up

Placing the cast-off ends in the centre, stitch the petals edge to edge.

With red tapestry yarn, stitch a long, straight stitch in the centre of each flower petal, radiating out from the middle of the flower.

Run a gathering stitch all round the edge of the centre piece, place the button inside and pull up tightly to gather up and enclose the button.

Stitch the flower centre firmly in place.

To brighten up the house, stitch flowers to cushions, curtain tie-backs or place mats. Choose bright coloured yarn for the main part of the flower. The variation shown here is orange but you could make up flowers in red, yellow, purple and white, too.

Hibiscus

Materials:

4-ply wool or wool-blend yarn, deep salmon
   pink and red

Tapestry wool, orange

Acrylic double knitting bouclé yarn, yellow

Measurements:

Finished flower measures 11cm (4³/₈in) across

Instructions:

With salmon pink yarn and size 3.00mm
(UK 11; US 2) needles, cast on 4 sts.

Row 1: inc 1, k to end.

Row 2: inc 1, p to end.

Rep rows 1 and 2 twice more (10 sts).

Row 7: sl 1, k to end.

Row 8: sl 1 knitwise, p to last st, k1.

Rep rows 7 and 8 twice more.

Cut yarn, slip to base of left-hand needle or
transfer to spare needle.

Make 4 more petals in the same way; do not
break yarn on last petal.

Next row: k to end, knit across all sts of 4
reserved petals (50 sts).

Next row: p; break yarn.

Next row: join in red yarn * k2tog, rep from *
to end (25 sts).

Next row: p.

Next row: * k2tog, rep from * to last st, k1
(13 sts).

Next row: * p2tog, rep from * to last st, p1.

Cut yarn, leaving a tail and thread this through
rem 7 sts.

Pistil

With orange yarn and two double-pointed
needles, cast on 2 sts.

Row 1: k2; do not turn but slide sts to other end
of needle.

Needles:

1 pair 3.00mm (UK 11; US 2) knitting needles,

Tapestry needle

Rep this row until work measures 3 cm (1¼in);
break off yarn and join in yellow.

Next row: k.

Next row: inc in each st (4 sts).

Next row: inc 1, k to end (5 sts).

Rep last row once more.

Next row: k.

Next row: cast off 1, k to end.

Rep last row until there are 2 sts.

Cast off; break yarn, leaving a tail.

Making up

Bring the two edges of the flower petals
together, stitch the lower parts of the two end
petals together; then run a gathering stitch
along the base of the petals and pull up tightly
to gather, trapping the base of the pistil in
the centre. Stitch
securely
in place.

Fold over
the yellow
part of
the pistil
and
stitch
to form
a neat
bobble.

Stitch a hibiscus to the ends of a silk scarf, pin to the lapel of a jacket, or use to decorate a hat for a special occasion. The alternative below has been made using a bamboo yarn in subtle shades of peach and apricot. The pistil is made in the same apricot yarn. Using this different yarn type but the same needles, the flower ends up slightly larger, measuring 13cm (5⅛in) at its widest point.

Clematis

Materials:

Felting yarn, pure wool, deep violet
Eyelash yarn, 100% polyester, white
Scissors

Needles:

1 pair 3.00mm (UK 11; US 2) knitting needles
Tapestry needle

Measurements:

Finished flower measures 14cm (5½in) across

Instructions:

Petal (make 8)

With deep violet yarn and size 3.00mm
(UK 11; US 2) needles, cast on 7 sts.

Row 1 (WS): p3, inc 2, p3 (9 sts).

Row 2: k3, p3, k3.

Row 3: p3, inc 1, k1, inc 1, p3 (11 sts).

Row 4: k3, p5, k3.

Row 5: p3, k5, p3.

Rep rows 4 and 5 once more.

Row 8: as row 4.

Row 9: p3, k1, sl1, k2tog, psso, k1, p3 (9 sts).

Row 10: k3, p3, k3.

Row 11: p3, sl1, k2tog, psso, p3 (7 sts).

Row 12: k3, p1, k3.

Row 13: p2, p3tog, p2 (5 sts).

Row 14: k.

Row 15: p1, p3tog, p1 (3 sts).

Row 16: k.

Row 17: p3tog; break yarn and fasten off.

Making up

Join four petals together at the corners, using
tails of yarn. Thread a long tail of yarn in a
running stitch through the base of each petal,
then pull up the thread to gather tightly. Fasten
off. Repeat with the other four petals. Place
one group of four on top of the other and stitch
them together.

To make the centre, wind eyelash yarn around
two fingers about twelve times. Tie yarn around
the centre to form a small bundle, then pull
the ends through the flower centre and secure.
Trim with scissors.

Make a statement by pinning one or
more clematis to a hatband, or use to
decorate a bag or purse. The alternative here
has been made up in a very pale pink bamboo yarn;
the same yarn has been used to make a frayed flower centre.

Sweet William

Materials:

4-ply cotton yarn, red, pink and white

Needles:

Set of 5 double-pointed 3.00mm (UK 11; US 2)
   knitting needles
Tapestry needle

Measurements:

Finished flower measures 4.5cm (1¾in) across

Instructions:

With white yarn and size 3.00mm (UK 11; US
2) double-pointed needles, cast on 10 sts and
distribute between four needles as follows: four
on one needle and two each on the other
three needles.

Round 1: k; cut yarn.

Round 2: join in red yarn and k 1 round.

Round 3: inc in every stitch (20 sts).

Round 4: inc in every stitch (50 sts); cut yarn.

Row 5: join in pink yarn, k 8, turn.

Next row: k.

Cast off; cut yarn and fasten off.

Rejoin yarn to next st in round and rep from
Row 5 four times more.

Making up

Weave in red and white yarn ends on the wrong
side of the flower.

Run each pink yarn end down the side of the
petal, neatening the petal edges as you do
this, and fasten at the back of the work.

This tiny flower makes a lovely brooch. You could also stitch one or more to a hair slide or alice band for a pretty hair decoration, or attach shoe clips to decorate a plain pair of shoes, as shown here. Vary the design by using different combinations of the three colours.

Poppy

Materials:
Chunky acrylic yarn, red
Linen double knitting yarn, black
Round button, 22mm (8⅝in)

Needles:
1 pair 2.25mm (UK 13; US 1) knitting needles
1 pair 3.25mm (UK 10; US 3) knitting needles
Tapestry needle

Measurements:
Finished flower measures 12cm (4¾in) across

Instructions:

Petal (make 4)
With red chunky yarn and size 3.25mm (UK 10;
US 3) needles, cast on 13 sts.
Row 1: k all sts tbl.
Row 2: sl 1, k11, turn, leaving rem stitches on
needle.
Row 3: k11, turn.
Rep row 3 seven more times.
Row 11: k10, k2tog.
Row 12: sl1, k9, k2tog.
Row 13: k to end.
Rep last row 5 times.
Row 19: k4, sl 1, k2tog, psso, k4.
Row 20: k.
Row 21: k3, sl 1, k2tog, psso, k3.
Row 22: k.
Row 23: k2, sl 1, k2tog, psso, k2.
Row 24: k.
Row 25: k1, sl 1, k2tog, psso, k1.
Row 26: sl 1, k2tog, psso; fasten off.

Centre
With black linen yarn and 2.25mm (UK 13; US 1)
needles, cast on 6 sts.
Row 1: k.
Row 2: inc 1, k to last st, inc 1 (8 sts).

Row 3: inc 1, k to last st, inc 1 (10 sts).
Knit 10 rows.
Row 14: k2tog, k to last 2 sts, k2tog (8 sts).
Row 14: k2tog, k to last 2 sts, k2tog (6 sts).
Cast off.

Stamens
With black linen yarn and 2.25mm needles, cast
on 10 sts.
Row 1: cast off, leaving 1 st on needle.
Row 2: cast on 9 sts.
Row 3: cast off, leaving 1 st on needle.
Rep rows 2 and
3 six times
more.
Cast off
rem st.

Making up

Stitch the petals together, arranging them so that the pointed bases meet in the centre and each straight side edge overlaps its neighbour by about 2mm (¹/₈in).

Stitch a running thread around the edge of the centre piece, place the button inside and pull up the yarn to gather; fasten off securely.

Join the two ends of the row of stamens, then run a thread along the base and pull up to gather. Stitch to the centre of the flower and stitch the covered button on top.

Big and bold, use the red poppy as a corsage on a plain coat, or pin it to a hat when you want to make a statement. For an alternative, use a pure wool double knitting yarn in pink, with a grey wool centre, creating a more subtle effect. Using a lighter yarn with the same size needles produces a slightly smaller flower (this one is 11cm/4³/₈in in diameter).

Chrysanthemum

Materials:
Wool and cotton double knitting yarn,
mustard yellow

Needles:
1 pair 3.25mm (UK 10; US 3) knitting needles
Tapestry needle

Measurements:
Finished flower measures approximately 12cm
(4¾in) across

Instructions:
With mustard yellow yarn and size 3.25mm (UK
10; US 3) needles, cast on 22 sts.

Row 1: k all sts tbl.

Row 2: k all sts tbl.

Row 3: cast off, leaving 1 st on needle.

Row 4: cast on 21 sts.

Row 5: k all sts tbl.

Rep rows 3-5 13 times more, then row 3 once.

Next row: cast on 19 sts.

Next row: k all sts tbl.

Next row: cast off, leaving 1 st on needle.

Rep last three rows 5 times.

Next row: cast on 15 sts.

Next row: k all sts tbl.

Next row: cast off, leaving 1 st on needle.

Rep last three rows 5 times.

Next row: cast on 12 sts.

Next row: k all sts tbl.

Next row: cast off, leaving 1 st on needle.

Rep last three rows 5 times then cast off rem st,
break yarn and fasten off.

Making up
Stitch a gathering thread along the base of all
the petals and pull up tightly to gather. Form
some of the longer petals into loops, stitching
the end of each one securely to the centre of
the flower.

As an alternative, use a variegated cotton double knitting yarn and, using the instructions as a guide, make only twenty-eight petals in total, six of 16 sts, twelve of 13 sts, and ten of 10 sts. When making up, do not loop any of the petals.

Tulip

Materials:

Linen double knitting yarn, orange

2 yellow pipe cleaners, 23cm (9in)

Pure wool double knitting yarn, green

Measurements:

Finished flower measures
approximately 7cm (2¾in)
across and 31cm (12¼in) long

Instructions:

Petal (make 3)

With orange yarn and 3.25mm (UK 10; US 3)
needles, cast on 5 sts

Round 1: k.

Row 1: k each st tbl.

Row 2: k1, inc 1, k1, inc 1, k1 (7 sts).

Row 3: k.

Row 4: k2, inc 1, k1, inc 1, k2 (9 sts).

Row 5: k.

Row 6: k3, inc 1, k1, inc 1, k3 (11 sts).

Row 7: k.

Row 8: k4, inc 1, k1, inc 1, k4 (13 sts).

Row 9: k.

Row 10: k5, inc 1, k1, inc 1, k5 (15 sts).

Knit 8 rows.

Row 19: sl 1, k1, psso, k11, k2tog (13 sts).

Row 20: k.

Row 21: sl 1, k1, psso, k9, k2tog (11 sts).

Row 22: k.

Row 23: sl 1, k1, psso, k7, k2tog (9 sts).

Row 24: k.

Row 25: sl 1, k1, psso, k5, k2tog (7 sts).

Row 26: k.

Row 27: sl 1, k1, psso, k3, k2tog (5 sts).

Row 28: k.

Row 29: sl 1, k1, psso, k1, k2tog (3 sts).

Row 30: sl 1, k2tog, psso; fasten off.

Needles:

1 pair 3.25mm (UK 10, US 3)
knitting needles

1 pair double-pointed knitting
needles, 3.00mm (UK11; US2)

Tapestry needle

Stalk

With green yarn and two double-pointed
needles, cast on 5 sts.

Row 1: k5; do not turn but slide sts to other end
of needle.

Rep this row until work measures 21cm (8¼in);
fasten off.

Making up

Fold over 5mm (¼in) at either end of one of
the pipe cleaners and slip it inside the stalk.
Stitch the ends of the stalk closed. Stitch
the top of the stalk to the base of one of the
petals. Cut the second pipe cleaner into three
equal lengths, fold each one in half and attach
to the top of the stalk to create
stamens. Wrap the
two remaining
petals around
the first and
stitch.

34

Tulips come in lots of lovely colours; choose your favourite. Arrange single tulips on a shelf or across the top of a mirror or picture frame, or display in a vase.

Periwinkle

Materials:
Pure wool 4-ply yarn, blue and ivory
Glass seed beads, yellow
Sewing thread, white or yellow

Needles:
1 pair 2.25mm (UK 13; US 1) knitting needles
Tapestry needle
Stitch holder
Sewing needle

Measurements:
Finished flower measures 7cm (2¾in) across

Instructions:

Petal (make 5)
With blue yarn and size 2.25mm (UK 13; US 1) needles, cast on 12 sts.

Row 1: (k1, sl 1 purlwise with yarn at back of work) six times.

Rep last row 15 times; break off yarn.

Join in ivory yarn and rep row 1 six times more.

Break off yarn, leaving a long tail; transfer to a stitch holder.

Making up
Each petal needs to be finished off before joining to make up the flower. Thread the tail of yarn on to a tapestry needle. Carefully slip stitches off the stitch holder and pull apart the two sides of the petal, separating the stitches. Thread the yarn through each stitch in turn then turn the petal inside out and pull up the yarn to gather the base of the petal.

Join the petals at the centre, then sew on a little cluster of eight seed beads.

These little woollen flowers have a very retro feel. Pin them to a cardigan, a linen jacket or woolly hat. You can also make a plain blue version.

Anemone

Materials:

Lambswool and mohair double knitting yarn,
    purple and black

Eyelash yarn, white

Round button, 12mm (½in)

Needles:

1 pair knitting needles, 2.75mm (UK 12; US 2)

Tapestry needle

Measurements:

Finished flower measures approximately
    9cm (3½in) across

Instructions:

Petal (make 6)

With purple yarn and size 2.75mm (UK 12; US 2)
needles, cast on 4 sts.

Row 1: k all sts tbl.

Row 2: inc 1, k to end.

Rep last row until there are 10 sts.

Knit 10 rows.

Next row: k1, sl 1, k1, psso, k4, k2tog, k1.

Next row: k1, sl 1, k1, psso, k2, k2tog, k1.

Next row: k1, sl 1, k1, psso, k2tog, k1.

Next row: k2tog twice.

Next row: k2tog.

Fasten off.

Centre

With black yarn and size 2.75mm needles,
cast on 2 sts.

Row 1: inc 1, k to end.

Rep row 1 until there are 6 sts.

Knit 3 rows.

Next row: cast off 1, k to end.

Rep last row until there are 2 sts.

Cast off; break yarn and fasten off.

Making up

Position the petals so that cast-off end is at the
centre. Stitch the petals together, overlapping
each one.

Stitch a running thread around the edge of the
centre piece, place the button inside and pull
up the yarn to gather; fasten off securely.

Thread the tapestry needle with a length of
white eyelash yarn and overstitch the perimeter
of the covered button. Tease out a few of the
strands. Stitch the button to the flower centre.

Use the same yarn in red to make a perfect partner for the purple anemone. Pin or stitch one or more anemones to a plain sweater or scarf, or fasten to a length of ribbon to make a choker.

Cherry Blossom

Materials:
Bamboo double knitting yarn, very pale pink
Pearl stamens

Needles:
1 pair 3.00mm (UK 11; US 2) knitting needles
Tapestry needle

Measurements:
Finished flower measures 5cm (2in) across

Instructions:

Petal (make 5)
With pale pink yarn and size 3.00mm
(UK 11; US 2) needles, cast on 5 sts.
Row 1: k4, turn, leaving rem st on needle.
Row 2: p3, turn, leaving rem st on needle.
Row 3: k3, turn.
Row 4: p3, turn.
Row 5: k4.
Row 6: p2tog, p1, p2tog (3 sts).
Row 7: k1, k2tog, psso.
Fasten off.

Making up
Join the petals at the centre, inserting stamens
and securing them with a few stitches.

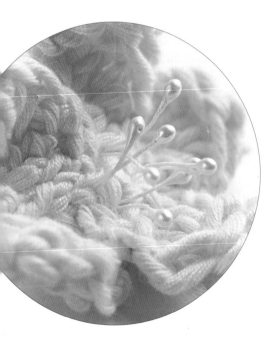

Opposite
*The perfect choice for a bridesmaid, stitch
one or more blossoms to a hair slide or clip
for a pretty hair decoration, or to a length
of ribbon to make a choker or wrist corsage.
For an alternative, use double knitting
cotton yarn in a bright pink and, instead
of stamens, stitch a few seed beads in the
centre of the flower.*

Arum Lily

Materials:

Double knitting cotton yarn, white
Pure wool double knitting yarn, orange
Pure wool double knitting yarn, green

Measurements:

Finished flower measures 18cm (7¹⁄₈in) long,
   including stem

Instructions:

With white yarn and size 3.00mm double-
pointed needles, cast on 8 sts and distribute
between four needles.

Knit 3 rounds.

Round 4: inc in each st (16 sts).

Knit 3 rounds.

Round 8: (inc 1, k3) 4 times (20 sts).

Knit 2 rounds.

Round 11: (inc 1, k4) 4 times (24 sts).

Knit 2 rounds.

Round 14: inc 1, k5) 4 times (28 sts).

Knit 2 rounds.

Round 17: (inc 1, k6) 4 times (32 sts).

Knit 8 rounds.

Round 26: (inc 1, k7) 4 times (36 sts).

Round 27: (inc 1, k8) 4 times (40 sts).

Round 28: (inc 1, k9) 4 times (44 sts).

Round 29: (inc 1, k10) 4 times (48 sts).

Round 30: (inc 1, k11) 4 times (52 sts).

Round 31: (inc 1, k12) 4 times (56 sts).

Round 32: (inc 1, k13) 4 times (60 sts).

Purl 1 round.

Cast off knitwise.

Spadix

With orange yarn and size 3.00mm needles,
cast on 20 sts.

Row 1: k all sts tbl.

Row 2: k16, turn.

Needles:

Set of 5 double-pointed knitting needles,
   3.00mm (UK 11; US 2)

1 pair 3.00mm (UK 11; US 2) knitting needles

Row 3: sl 1, k to end.

Row 4: k12, turn.

Row 5: sl 1, k to end.

Row 6: k to end.

Knit 6 rows.

Cast off.

Stem

With green yarn and two double-pointed
needles, cast on 5 sts.

Row 1: k5; do not turn but slide sts to other end
of needle.

Rep this row until work measures 6.5cm (2½in);
fasten off.

Making up

Stitch the cast-on and cast-off edges of the spadix together to form a tube. Stitch the base to the top of the stem. Insert into the flower and secure at the flower base.

Place on a mantelpiece or dressing table, or arrange several in a glass bowl. To create an alternative lily, use a pure wool double knitting yarn in a deep pink-violet shade for the main part of the flower.

Daisy

Materials:

Cotton double knitting yarn, white
Acrylic double knitting bouclé yarn, yellow
Round button, 3cm (1¼in)

Needles:

1 pair 2.25mm (UK 13; US 1) knitting needles
Tapestry needle

Measurements:

Finished flower measures 15cm (6in) across

Instructions:

Petals (made in one piece)

With white cotton yarn and size 2.25mm
(UK 13; US 1) needles, cast on 14 sts.

Row 1: k all sts tbl.

Row 2: k11, turn.

Row 3: k to end.

Row 4: k.

Row 5: cast off 12, k rem st.

Row 6: k2, cast on 12.

Rep rows 1–6 14 times, omitting row 6 on final
rep and casting off last 2 sts instead.

Break yarn and fasten off.

Centre

With yellow bouclé yarn and size 2.25mm
needles, cast on 6 sts.

Row 1: k.

Row 2: inc 1, k to last st, inc 1 (8 sts).

Row 3: k.

Row 4: inc 1, k to last st, inc 1 (10 sts).

Row 5: k.

Row 6: inc 1, k to last st, inc 1 (12 sts).

Knit 8 rows.

Row 15: sl 1, k1, psso, k8, k2tog (10 sts).

Row 16: k.

Row 17: sl 1, k1, psso, k6, k2tog (8 sts).

Row 18: k.

Row 19: sl 1, k1, psso, k4, k2tog (6 sts).

Cast off.

Making up

Join the two ends of the petals to form a ring.
Stitch a gathering thread along the base of all
the petals and pull up tightly to gather.

Stitch a running thread around the edge of the
centre piece, place the button inside and pull
up the yarn to gather; fasten off securely.

Stitch the covered button to the centre of
the flower.

Use the white daisy to decorate a summer hat or beach bag. Use blue yarn to make a Michaelmas daisy, or create a customised daisy in your favourite colour.

Rose

Materials:
Pure wool double knitting yarn, red

Needles:
Pair of knitting needles, 3.00mm (UK 11; US 2)
Tapestry needle

Measurements:
Finished flower measures 8cm (3¹/₈in) across

Instructions:

Petal (make 6)
With red yarn and size 3.00mm (UK 11; US 2)
needles, cast on 2 sts.
Row 1: inc in each st (4 sts).
Row 2: inc 1, k to end.
Row 3: inc 1, p to last st, k1.
Rep rows 2 and 3 until there are 10 sts.
Knit 8 rows.
Next row: k2tog, k6, k2tog (8 sts).
Next row: k2tog, p4, k2tog.
Next row: k2tog, k2, K2tog.
Next row: k2tog twice.
Next row: k2tog.
Fasten off.

Flower centre
With red yarn and size 3.00mm needles, cast
on 108 sts.
Row 1: k all sts tbl.
Row 2: p2tog to end of row (54 sts).
Row 3: k.
Row 4: (p2tog, p4) to end of row (45 sts).
Row 5: k.
Row 6: (p2tog, p3) to end of row (36 sts).
Row 7: k.
Row 8: p2tog to end of row (18 sts).

Row 9: k.
Row 10: p2tog to end of row (9 sts).
Break yarn and thread through rem sts.

Making up
Curl the centre into a spiral and pull up the tail
of yarn to gather the base, then secure it with a
few stitches.

Stitch petals one at a time around the centre,
with the cast-off edge of each petal at the base
of the flower.

A rose makes the perfect corsage on a coat, jacket or sweater. A cluster of roses would make a pretty decoration for a hat or bag. Pink yarn also makes a lovely rose – but roses come in all colours, so choose your favourite.

Acknowledgements

Thanks to Julieta Brandao of knitshop.co.uk for supplying yarns for this book, particularly the delicious silks; also to Jamieson & Smith for Shetland wool yarns; and to Coats Patons and Stylecraft for some of the more unusual yarns.
Many thanks to Managing Editor Sophie Kersey for her patience and to Roz Dace for commissioning me to do the book in the first place. Thanks also to Gavin and Roddy for their stylish photography.

You are invited to visit the author's website:
susieatthecircus.typepad.com

Publishers' Note

If you would like more information on knitting techniques, try:
Beginner's Guide to Knitting by Alison Dupernex,
Search Press, 2004;
The Compendium of Knitting Techniques by Betty Barnden,
Search Press, 2008 and
Twenty to Make: Knitted Cakes by Susan Penny,
Search Press, 2008